All About Kylian Mbappé: A Kid's Guide to the Young Football Star

Knowledge Books For Kids, Volume 86

Shah Rukh

Published by Shah Rukh, 2025.

ALL ABOUT KYLIAN MBAPPÉ: A KID'S GUIDE TO THE YOUNG FOOTBALL STAR

First edition. June 27, 2025.

ISBN: 979-8231428687

Written by Shah Rukh.

Table of Contents

Prologue

Kylian Mbappé wasn't born a football star—he became one with hard work, big dreams, and incredible speed. From the streets of Bondy, a small town near Paris, to the biggest stadiums in the world, Mbappé's journey is nothing short of amazing. He was just a kid with a ball, a lot of energy, and a heart full of passion.

This book will take you through the exciting life of one of the world's youngest football legends. You'll learn how Mbappé chased his goals, overcame challenges, and inspired millions—proving that no dream is too big if you're willing to run fast enough to catch it.

Chapter 1: The Boy Who Loved the Ball

When Kylian Mbappé was just a little boy, he didn't care much about toys or cartoons like many kids his age. What truly made him happy was a soccer ball. From the moment he could walk, he wanted to kick, dribble, and run with the ball. Even before he could say full sentences, he was already trying out new tricks with his tiny feet. He loved how the ball felt when he tapped it softly with his toes or when he kicked it across the room. It was like the soccer ball was his best friend, always there to play with him and never letting him feel bored. While other kids played video games or rode bikes, Kylian would be outside, practicing his footwork on the pavement, on the grass, or even inside his home.

He didn't wait for special lessons or training. His playground was anywhere there was a bit of space, and his imagination turned those spaces into giant stadiums filled with cheering fans. Kylian's favorite thing was pretending he was one of the big football stars he watched on TV. He would shout out the names of famous players as he scored pretend goals and celebrated like a champion. Sometimes he even wore costumes or old jerseys just to feel like he was already a superstar. The ball followed him everywhere. He would eat quickly just to have more time to play. He would carry the ball with him to school, to the grocery store, or even to visit relatives. It was almost like the ball was a part of him.

Kylian's family noticed this love right away. His father, who worked as a football coach, saw that this wasn't just a phase. His mother, who had been a handball player herself, could tell that Kylian had something special. They didn't force him to train or push him to be the best. Instead, they encouraged his passion by cheering for him, guiding him gently, and letting him follow his heart. His bedroom walls were covered with posters of famous players like Cristiano Ronaldo and Zinedine Zidane. He would watch their games again and again, studying every move they made. He wasn't just a boy who liked football—he was a boy who breathed it, dreamed it, and lived for it every single day.

Every afternoon, as soon as school was over, Kylian would rush home, toss his backpack aside, and dash out to practice. Whether it was sunny, cloudy, or even a bit rainy, nothing could stop him. He would make goals out of shoes, fences, or cones and challenge himself to score in as many creative ways as possible. If he missed a shot, he didn't get upset. Instead, he would try again and again until he got it right. His determination was as strong as his love for the game. He didn't mind falling or getting muddy. In fact, he thought it was fun, because it meant he was getting better.

Even when he was just six or seven, people around the neighborhood started noticing his skills. They would stop and watch him play, amazed at how fast and skillful he was for such a young child. Some even called him a little genius with the ball. But Kylian didn't care about compliments or attention. He played for the joy, for the challenge, and because every time his foot touched the ball, he felt like he was flying. He loved spinning around defenders, shooting into pretend goals, and imagining the crowd roaring with excitement. His heart raced not because he was tired, but because he was having the time of his life.

At night, he would go to bed holding his ball, sometimes falling asleep with his shoes still on. In his dreams, he was scoring goals in packed stadiums and holding up golden trophies. These dreams weren't just stories in his head—they were goals he truly believed in. He never once doubted that he could become a professional footballer. To him, it wasn't a far-off wish—it was something real, something he was working toward every single day. Even when grown-ups told him it was hard, or that only a few kids make it, Kylian didn't let that worry him. He just smiled, nodded, and went back to kicking his ball.

His love for the ball wasn't just about fun; it was also about expression. When he was happy, he played faster. When he was sad, he played harder. The ball helped him show his feelings, even the ones he didn't know how to say out loud. It was like a magical connection between his heart and the world. His bond with football was more than just a hobby—it was the rhythm of his life. And the best part was, he never got tired of it. The more he played, the more he loved it.

As he grew older, Kylian's love only deepened. He didn't just watch games; he studied them. He looked at how players moved, passed, and worked together. He started asking questions, wanting to understand strategies and positions. This curiosity made him even better. Coaches began to notice his talent and discipline. But what stood out the most was the spark in his eyes every time he saw a ball. He didn't care about being famous. He cared about getting better, playing harder, and learning more. That pure love made him different from many others.

From kicking a ball around the house to practicing in local parks, from pretending to be a star to actually becoming one, it all started because a little boy fell in love with a ball. His story shows that when you truly love something and give it your all, amazing things can happen. That's how Kylian Mbappé began—just a boy with a ball, a dream, and a heart full of passion that couldn't be stopped.

Chapter 2: Growing Up in Bondy

Kylian Mbappé grew up in a place called Bondy, which is a town just outside of Paris, the capital of France. Bondy wasn't a fancy or rich place—it was a neighborhood where many families worked very hard to earn a living. The buildings weren't tall skyscrapers or shiny glass towers. Instead, there were apartment blocks, local shops, parks, and lots of playgrounds. For many kids in Bondy, football wasn't just a game—it was a way to have fun, stay active, and dream of something bigger. Bondy had its struggles, like not having enough opportunities or facing challenges with jobs and schools, but it also had heart, energy, and strong community spirit. That's where Kylian's journey began, in a neighborhood full of noise, movement, and everyday stories.

From a young age, Kylian felt connected to Bondy in a very special way. It wasn't just where he lived—it was the place that shaped who he was. He played on the same streets as other kids, kicking a ball around in the yard, the park, or even between buildings. The people in the neighborhood were used to seeing groups of children running around with soccer balls at their feet, but even then, Kylian stood out. His speed, focus, and footwork made people stop and watch. But beyond his skills, it was his attitude that made a difference. He was polite, cheerful, and determined, always smiling and encouraging his friends during games.

Kylian's family was a big part of his life in Bondy. His dad, Wilfried Mbappé, was not just a football coach but also someone who believed in teaching kids discipline, teamwork, and self-belief. His mom, Fayza Lamari, was a former handball player who knew what it meant to train hard and never give up. Together, they created a loving home where Kylian was taught to respect others, stay humble, and believe in his dreams. They didn't give him everything he asked for, but they gave him what mattered—support, guidance, and a chance to chase what he loved most: football.

Bondy had its own local football club, and that's where Kylian really began to shine. His father helped train the young players, and Kylian joined the team when he was very small. Even though the field wasn't fancy and the equipment was simple, the passion was real. He would arrive early to practice and leave late, always wanting to do more. He treated every session like a chance to grow. While other kids sometimes complained about running or drills, Kylian did everything with excitement. He loved every part of it, from warming up to scoring goals. The coaches noticed that he listened carefully, followed instructions, and tried his best, no matter what.

At school in Bondy, Kylian was like many other kids. He studied, played during recess, and had friends. But his classmates knew he was different because of how seriously he took football. He would talk about the game all the time, draw pictures of famous players, and even come up with game strategies on paper. While some kids dreamed of being firefighters or astronauts, Kylian already had one dream and never changed it—he wanted to be a professional footballer. Teachers would sometimes smile and remind him to focus on his homework, but even they could see that his dream was more than just a wish. It was a goal he was working toward every single day.

Even though Bondy wasn't known as a place where stars were born, it gave Kylian everything he needed to become one. The streets taught him how to be quick and creative, the people taught him how to stay grounded, and his family taught him how to handle both success and failure. He wasn't raised in luxury, but he was raised with love and values that helped him grow into a kind and respectful person. The challenges around him didn't bring him down. Instead, they made him stronger and more focused. He learned to be thankful for what he had and to use every opportunity wisely.

The kids in Bondy looked up to Kylian, even when he was still young. They saw how fast he ran, how cleverly he moved the ball, and how excited he got after scoring a goal. But more than anything, they saw how much he cared. He would cheer for his teammates, share tips, and help others practice. He wasn't just trying to be the best—he was trying to lift everyone around him. That's something very special, especially in a town where people often had to work twice as hard to be noticed. Kylian never acted like he was better than anyone. He knew where he came from and stayed connected to that place, even as he started to grow more popular.

When football scouts from big academies started visiting Bondy to watch Kylian play, it felt like something magical was happening. People in the neighborhood were excited and proud. Everyone believed he had something rare. But Kylian never let the attention change him. He still went to training like always, helped his mom with chores, and laughed with his friends. He never showed off or bragged. That humble attitude came from growing up in a place like Bondy, where people appreciate hard work and real effort more than flashy things.

Even after Kylian moved on to bigger clubs and started playing with top teams, he never forgot about his hometown. He visited Bondy often, supported local causes, and stayed close to the community. He knew that his roots were important, and he wanted to be a role model for other kids growing up in the same streets. He wanted them to know that big dreams can come from small places and that greatness can begin with just a ball, a dream, and a lot of heart. For Kylian, Bondy wasn't just his past—it was a part of who he would always be.

That little town, with its simple streets and strong spirit, raised one of the greatest football stars in the world. And even though he now plays in huge stadiums with fans from all over the globe, the lessons Kylian learned growing up in Bondy still guide him every day—lessons about family, hard work, staying kind, and never forgetting where you came from.

Chapter 3: Dreams of the World Cup

Ever since Kylian Mbappé was a little boy, one dream always stood out above the rest—the dream of playing in the FIFA World Cup. For many children who love football, the World Cup is the biggest, most exciting event they can imagine. It's where the best players from all over the globe come together to compete for the most treasured trophy in the sport. Kylian didn't just want to watch the World Cup on TV—he wanted to be on that field, wearing his country's jersey, and scoring goals for France. This dream was in his heart from the time he first kicked a ball. He imagined what it would feel like to run onto the pitch with the crowd cheering, to hear the national anthem play, and to know that millions of people were watching. Every time he trained, played, or practiced, this dream pushed him forward like a powerful engine inside him.

At home in Bondy, Kylian would talk about the World Cup all the time. He would collect stickers of players, memorize the history of the tournaments, and study the matches from years before. He knew about the legends—Pelé, Maradona, Zidane—and he wanted to follow in their footsteps. He didn't just want to be part of the World Cup; he wanted to leave a mark, to do something unforgettable. He would practice celebrating goals the way famous players did and dream about lifting the golden trophy above his head, surrounded by teammates. Even when he was playing in the streets or parks, he would pretend it was the final game of the World Cup, imagining the crowd roaring with every move he made.

His bedroom was filled with posters, not just of club stars, but of players who had shined in the World Cup. He knew their stories, their moments of glory, and even their mistakes. These stories taught him that the path to the World Cup wasn't easy. It took years of hard work, patience, and strength to get there. That didn't scare Kylian—it motivated him. He understood that being part of something so big would mean sacrificing time, staying focused, and training with purpose. While some kids were out relaxing, Kylian was practicing penalties, studying matches, or jogging to build stamina. He was building himself into the kind of player the world would cheer for.

As Kylian grew older and joined better teams, the dream stayed just as strong. Even though he was already doing amazing things at the club level, the thought of the World Cup kept him humble and hungry. He believed that no trophy was as important or magical as that one. Representing France on the biggest stage was more than a goal—it was something he felt in his soul. Every time he wore the blue jersey of France, he felt a wave of pride. He wasn't just playing for himself or his team—he was playing for his whole country, for the people who believed in him, and for the kids in places like Bondy who dared to dream like he once had.

Then came 2018, a year that would change everything. Kylian was only 19 years old, still a teenager, but he was chosen to play in the World Cup for France. It was like a dream coming true right before his eyes. But Kylian didn't let the pressure get to him. Instead of being nervous, he was filled with joy and determination. He had imagined this moment so many times that it felt natural to be there. He trained hard, listened to his coaches, and gave his all in every match. He played with confidence, speed, and passion, scoring important goals and making incredible runs. People around the world started talking about him, amazed by how fearless and talented he was.

In the final match of the 2018 World Cup, Kylian scored a goal that made history. He became the youngest French player ever to score in a World Cup final and the second teenager in history—after Pelé—to score in such a big moment. France won the match, and Kylian helped bring the trophy home. It was the exact dream he had been chasing for years, now turned into reality. He stood on the field with a smile as bright as the sun, holding the golden trophy, with fireworks lighting up the sky. It was a moment that millions of people watched live, and it was something Kylian would never forget.

But for Kylian, the World Cup wasn't just about winning. It was also about inspiring others. After that victory, he became a hero to kids everywhere, especially those from small neighborhoods and simple homes. He showed that with love, hard work, and belief, anything is possible. He reminded the world that dreams can come true, no matter where you start. Kylian didn't stop dreaming after winning. In fact, he started dreaming even bigger. He wanted to return to future World Cups and do even more. He wanted to keep making people proud and continue spreading joy through football.

In 2022, Kylian returned to the World Cup stage once again, this time as one of the biggest stars in the world. People expected great things from him, and he did not disappoint. He played with heart, scoring goals and leading his team to another final. Even though France didn't win that time, Kylian amazed everyone by scoring a hat trick in the final—three goals in one of the most important games ever played. It was a rare and brilliant performance that showed the world just how special he was. He may not have lifted the trophy that day, but he won the hearts of millions.

Now, Kylian is already thinking about the next World Cup. He knows the road will be tough, but he's ready to face it with the same energy, excitement, and love for the game that he had as a kid in Bondy. He wants to help his country again, be a leader on and off the field, and create new memories that will last forever. For Kylian Mbappé, the World Cup isn't just a tournament. It's the place where dreams begin, where legends are made, and where the spirit of football shines the brightest. And as long as he's playing, he will keep dreaming of lifting that trophy once more, with joy in his heart and the whole world watching.

Chapter 4: Training with Dad

When Kylian Mbappé was growing up in Bondy, one of the most important people in his life was his dad, Wilfried Mbappé. His father wasn't just his parent—he was also his very first coach and one of the biggest reasons why Kylian became the incredible football player he is today. From the very beginning, training with his dad wasn't like regular practice. It was something special, something filled with love, lessons, and the dream of one day reaching the top of the football world. Even before Kylian joined any big team, his training journey had already started at home, in parks, and on local fields, with his dad guiding him every step of the way.

Wilfried Mbappé worked at the local football club in Bondy and was known in the neighborhood for being a caring but serious coach. He believed in discipline and doing things properly, and he wanted to teach Kylian not just how to play, but how to understand the game deeply. Their training sessions weren't always easy, but they were always filled with meaning. They didn't have fancy equipment or giant stadiums, but that didn't matter. What mattered was the effort and focus they put into every minute of practice. Kylian listened closely to every instruction, even when he was tired or when the drills were tough. He knew his dad wasn't just teaching him football—he was preparing him for life.

Every day after school or on weekends, Kylian and his dad would head to the nearby field. Sometimes it was sunny, sometimes it was cold, and sometimes it was muddy or windy, but they always showed up. Kylian would carry his football and a water bottle, and his dad would bring cones, markers, and ideas for new exercises. They practiced everything—dribbling through tight spaces, shooting with both feet, passing with accuracy, sprinting with the ball, and learning how to stay calm under pressure. Even when Kylian made mistakes, his dad never yelled. Instead, he explained what went wrong and how to fix it. His voice was patient but firm, and Kylian respected that deeply.

Training with his dad wasn't just about the physical parts of football. Wilfried also taught Kylian how to think like a footballer. He would ask him questions like, "Why did you make that move?" or "What would you do if a defender came from your left?" These questions helped Kylian learn to make smart decisions on the field. His dad helped him understand that football isn't just about running fast or kicking hard—it's about using your mind, staying calm, and working together with your teammates. These were the kinds of lessons that helped Kylian become more than just a good player; they helped him become a great one.

Sometimes their training sessions included fun challenges. Kylian loved when his dad turned practice into games. They would count how many times he could juggle the ball without it touching the ground or see how quickly he could complete a set of skills without losing control. These games made training enjoyable and exciting. Even though Kylian was serious about football, he never stopped having fun with it. His dad knew that fun was important, too—it kept the passion alive and made every session something Kylian looked forward to.

There were also days when training was really hard. Maybe Kylian was tired from school, or maybe he was frustrated because he couldn't get a new skill right. On those days, his dad didn't let him give up. He would encourage him to push a little harder, try one more time, or believe in himself even when things felt impossible. He reminded Kylian that true champions don't quit when things get tough—they keep going. This kind of encouragement helped build Kylian's mental strength, which would later help him during tough matches in front of thousands of fans.

Their bond grew stronger with every training session. Kylian knew his dad believed in him completely. That belief gave him confidence. It made him feel like he could accomplish anything as long as he stayed focused and worked hard. His dad didn't chase fame or money—he just wanted his son to be the best version of himself. That kind of support is rare and powerful, and Kylian knew how lucky he was to have it. Whenever he achieved something new, like getting chosen for a team or winning a game, he would look at his dad and smile, because he knew it was their shared victory.

As Kylian began to grow older and started training with bigger clubs, his dad continued to be by his side—not just as a coach, but as a supporter, a listener, and a mentor. He reminded Kylian to stay humble, to keep learning, and to never forget where he came from. Even when professionals were coaching him, Kylian still carried his father's lessons in his heart. He used the same focus, discipline, and work ethic he had learned during those early days of practice on the small Bondy fields. He never stopped remembering the voice of his dad cheering him on, correcting his footwork, or encouraging him to go one more round.

When Kylian finally made it to the world stage, playing for France and top clubs, many people praised his talent. But Kylian always gave credit to his dad. He knew that those early years of training weren't just about learning football—they were about learning how to be strong, how to face challenges, and how to stay kind and grounded. His dad helped shape him not just as an athlete, but as a person. That kind of training goes deeper than muscles and skills—it builds character.

Even now, when Kylian steps onto the pitch in front of huge crowds and cameras, a part of him still feels like that young boy training with his dad on the quiet field in Bondy. He remembers the long hours, the words of advice, and the feeling of being supported every step of the way. Training with his dad wasn't just the beginning of his football story—it was the foundation of everything he became. It was where his dreams took root, where his confidence grew, and where his heart for the game was shaped forever.

Chapter 5: Speed Like Lightning

One of the things that makes Kylian Mbappé truly unforgettable on the football field is his incredible speed. He doesn't just run fast—he runs like lightning, as if his feet have wings and the ground is pushing him forward with every step. People watching him for the first time are often amazed at how quickly he can zoom past defenders, chase down a ball, or break away from a group of players. It almost looks like he's in a race and he's the only one who knows where the finish line is. This kind of speed didn't just appear overnight. It came from years of practice, dedication, and a natural talent that few players in the world have ever matched. Kylian's speed has become one of his greatest weapons on the pitch, and it has helped him become one of the most feared and respected footballers around the world.

Even when Kylian was a little kid in Bondy, people noticed how fast he was. Whether he was racing his friends in the schoolyard or sprinting with a football at his feet, he always seemed to be just a little quicker than everyone else. While some kids needed time to pick up speed, Kylian seemed to explode forward from the very first step. His legs moved like powerful machines, and his balance was so good that even when he was running full speed, he could still keep perfect control of the ball. That kind of ability is extremely rare, especially in someone so young. Coaches would watch him glide across the field and shake their heads in amazement. It wasn't just that he was fast—it was that he made speed look so smooth and easy.

Kylian's father and other coaches understood early on that his speed was something special, and they worked to help him use it in the best way possible. He didn't just run straight ahead—he learned how to change directions quickly, how to slow down and then burst forward like a rocket, and how to time his runs so perfectly that defenders couldn't keep up. He practiced sprinting drills, quick turns, and short-distance bursts. These exercises helped him build strong leg muscles and fast reactions. He also studied how to move his body to gain speed without losing control. He learned how to lean forward, pump his arms, and take longer strides when chasing the ball. Even while running at full pace, he could spot his teammates, pass accurately, or take a powerful shot. That mix of speed and skill made him a nightmare for opponents.

When Kylian began playing against tougher teams, his speed became even more important. Defenders tried everything to stop him—they tugged at his shirt, blocked his path, or tried to predict where he would go. But Kylian always seemed one step ahead. He would slip through narrow spaces, dash past players before they could react, and suddenly appear in front of the goal. His bursts of acceleration were like flashes of lightning, catching everyone by surprise. Even when he had the ball at his feet, he could outrun players who weren't even touching it. That's something very few people in football history have been able to do. Usually, players are fast without the ball or skilled with it—but Kylian was both at once.

During the 2018 FIFA World Cup, the world saw just how fast Kylian really was. In a match against Argentina, he sprinted from his own half of the field all the way into the penalty area, leaving several defenders behind him. It was one of the most memorable moments of the tournament. People all over the globe couldn't believe how fast he moved. Some compared him to Olympic sprinters, while others said he looked like a superhero racing through a video game. His speed helped France win that match, and eventually, the whole tournament. It wasn't just fun to watch—it was game-changing. His ability to turn defense into attack in just a few seconds made him a constant threat.

But Kylian never let his talent go to his head. He knew that to keep his speed, he had to work harder than ever. He continued doing strength training, running drills, and recovery exercises to keep his muscles healthy. He followed a good diet, got enough sleep, and took care of his body. He knew that speed was like a gift, but it needed care and effort to stay sharp. He also practiced new moves that allowed him to combine speed with clever footwork. For example, he would learn how to fake out defenders with a sudden stop and then explode forward again. He didn't just want to be fast—he wanted to be unstoppable.

Other young players started trying to run like Kylian. They watched his videos, studied his techniques, and dreamed of having that same burst of energy. Coaches began teaching kids how to move like him, using him as an example of how powerful and effective speed could be in football. He inspired a whole generation to take sprinting seriously and showed them that you didn't need to be the tallest or strongest player to succeed—you could outrun your opponents with clever timing, sharp focus, and explosive energy.

What makes Kylian's speed even more exciting is the joy he brings when he's running. When he's dashing across the field with the wind in his face and the ball at his feet, he smiles. That smile shows how much he loves the game, how free he feels when he's moving, and how happy he is to be doing what he loves most. Fans watching from the stands or on TV feel that joy, too. It's like watching someone fly—not with wings, but with sheer passion and movement.

Kylian also uses his speed to help his teammates. If another player needs help, he'll rush back to defend. If someone is making a run, he'll race ahead to create space or offer support. His speed isn't just about getting goals—it's about being a team player, helping in every part of the game, and always giving 100%. That's what makes him such a complete footballer. He's not just a sprinter with a ball—he's a smart, generous, and hard-working athlete who knows how to use his speed to lift the whole team.

Even now, as one of the best players in the world, Kylian keeps working to stay fast. He knows that as players get older, they sometimes lose a bit of their speed. That's why he takes extra care to stretch, eat healthy, and keep his muscles in top shape. He studies other sports like track and field to learn new ways of improving his movement. He even watches his own match videos to find moments where he could've moved faster or smarter. That's the kind of dedication that keeps him at the top of his game.

Kylian Mbappé's speed is more than just a cool trick—it's a symbol of who he is. It shows his energy, his hunger, and his unstoppable desire to keep going, no matter the obstacle. When he runs, it's like time slows down for everyone else while he blazes forward. He makes the game more thrilling, more dynamic, and more alive. For kids watching him play, his speed is a reminder that you can chase your dreams with all your might, and if you run hard enough, you just might catch them.

Chapter 6: Joining the Monaco Team

When Kylian Mbappé was still a teenager, something amazing happened that brought him one big step closer to his dream of becoming a professional football star. He was invited to join the youth academy of AS Monaco, a famous football club in France that had a long history of developing young talent. This wasn't just any club—it was one of the top teams in the French league, known for giving young players a chance to shine on a big stage. For Kylian, joining the Monaco team was more than just a move to a new city or a new team—it was a life-changing moment that would shape his entire future in football.

Leaving his home in Bondy was not easy. He was still very young, and it meant saying goodbye to the familiar streets, his school friends, and the cozy apartment where he had grown up. But Kylian knew that opportunities like this didn't come around every day. He trusted his parents, especially his dad, who had helped guide him throughout his early training. They believed in his talent and knew he was ready for this next step. Even though it was a little scary to leave everything behind, Kylian was filled with excitement and determination. He saw it as a big adventure and a chance to prove what he could do.

When he arrived at Monaco's training center, Kylian couldn't believe how professional everything looked. The fields were perfect, the equipment was high-tech, and the coaches were experienced and smart. He was surrounded by other talented young players who all dreamed of becoming stars just like him. But even in this group of skilled athletes, Kylian stood out right away. His speed, his ball control, and his sharp thinking on the field impressed the coaches almost immediately. He wasn't just playing football—he was playing with heart, with energy, and with the kind of focus that you don't often see in someone so young.

The training sessions at Monaco were much harder and more serious than anything Kylian had experienced before. The drills were intense, the expectations were high, and the coaches didn't go easy on anyone. But Kylian didn't back down. He trained harder than ever, pushing himself to run faster, shoot better, and improve every part of his game. He stayed late after practice, worked on his weaknesses, and studied the game with the eyes of a future professional. He wanted to learn from everyone around him—from the coaches, from his teammates, and even from watching the older players on the senior team. Every day at Monaco felt like a chance to grow stronger, smarter, and more ready for the future he had always dreamed about.

Living at the academy also meant that Kylian had to become more independent. He had to manage his time, take care of his own responsibilities, and learn how to live away from his family. It wasn't always easy. There were days when he missed home, felt tired, or struggled with the pressure. But he never gave up. He reminded himself of why he was there and what he wanted to achieve. His love for football was so strong that it helped him stay focused, even when things were tough. He made new friends at the academy, players who shared the same passion and worked just as hard. They trained together, supported each other, and pushed one another to be better. Being part of a team like that made Kylian feel like he belonged.

After a while, Kylian's hard work began to pay off. He started to move up quickly through the youth ranks at Monaco, impressing the coaches with every game he played. He was scoring goals, making clever passes, and showing leadership far beyond his age. People around the club started talking about him, calling him a rising star. Scouts and journalists began to notice too. They saw that something special was happening—a young player was growing into a future legend right before their eyes. It wasn't long before the coaches decided to give him the biggest opportunity of all: a chance to play with the senior team.

Kylian made his professional debut for AS Monaco at just 16 years old. That's incredibly young to be playing at such a high level, but he handled it with confidence and grace. When he stepped onto the field for his first match, he wasn't nervous—he was thrilled. He had waited for this moment his entire life, and now it was finally real. The roar of the crowd, the lights of the stadium, the feeling of wearing the official jersey—it was everything he had imagined. And Kylian didn't disappoint. Even though he was one of the youngest players on the field, he played with the energy and skill of someone far older. His quick movements, sharp decisions, and fearless style instantly made him a fan favorite.

In the months that followed, Kylian's performances grew even stronger. He began scoring more goals, assisting his teammates, and becoming a key part of Monaco's attacking force. In the 2016–2017 season, something truly magical happened. Kylian helped lead Monaco to a Ligue 1 championship—the first time the club had won the league in nearly two decades. He was a big reason for their success, dazzling defenders with his pace, footwork, and clever moves. He scored important goals in both league matches and Champions League games, showing that he could perform not just in France but on the international stage too.

That season, Kylian's name became known across Europe. He wasn't just a promising young player anymore—he was a star in the making. Fans, players, and coaches all over the world began to talk about him. Clubs wanted to sign him, journalists wanted to interview him, and kids started pretending to be him on the playground. But through it all, Kylian stayed grounded. He always remembered where he came from, how hard he had worked, and who had helped him along the way. He thanked his family, respected his coaches, and stayed focused on improving even more.

Joining Monaco wasn't just the start of Kylian's professional career—it was the launchpad that helped him soar. It was the place where he transformed from a talented boy into a world-class footballer. It was where he learned to face challenges, handle pressure, and shine on the biggest stages. His time at Monaco showed the world that he wasn't just fast or skilled—he was brave, smart, and ready for greatness. And even after he moved on to bigger clubs, Monaco remained a special part of his journey—a place where a dreamer became a doer, and a young boy chasing a ball became one of the most exciting players the world had ever seen.

Chapter 7: Scoring His First Big Goal

Scoring his first big goal was a moment Kylian Mbappé would never forget—a moment that turned all his hard work, dreams, and training into something real and magical. For years, he had imagined what it would feel like to score a goal in a professional football match. He had dreamed about the roar of the crowd, the feeling of the ball hitting the back of the net, and the joy of running across the field with his teammates celebrating around him. That moment was always in his heart, pushing him to keep practicing even when he was tired, to keep running even when his legs ached, and to keep believing even when things seemed far away. And then, one day, that dream finally came true.

At just 17 years old, Kylian Mbappé was playing for AS Monaco, one of the top football clubs in France. He had already amazed everyone by becoming the youngest player to ever play for Monaco's first team, breaking the record set by legendary French footballer Thierry Henry. People were starting to pay attention to this lightning-fast teenager with incredible skills and a humble attitude. Coaches, fans, and reporters all wanted to see what he would do next. But even with all that attention, Kylian kept his head down and focused on doing what he loved most—playing football.

Then came the day when Kylian finally scored his first goal in a major professional match. It was February 2016, and Monaco was playing against a strong team. The stadium was buzzing with excitement, and Kylian was ready. He had come on as a substitute, full of energy and determination. He ran across the field with his usual speed and sharp movements, looking for the perfect moment. And then it happened. One of his teammates passed him the ball in just the right spot. Kylian took a touch to control it, kept his eyes on the goal, and struck the ball with power and precision. The goalkeeper tried to stop it, but it was too fast, too accurate. The ball flew into the net.

In that instant, time seemed to slow down. Kylian's heart leaped with joy as the crowd exploded into cheers. His teammates rushed toward him, hugging him, clapping him on the back, and smiling as if they had all just won a trophy. Kylian raised his arms, looking up into the stands, not quite believing what he had just done. It was more than a goal—it was a dream made real. It was the proof that all those hours of training, all those nights spent practicing alone, all the sacrifices he and his family had made, were worth it.

That goal wasn't just important because it was his first. It was important because it showed the world that Kylian Mbappé was ready for greatness. He had shown skill, courage, and confidence. He hadn't been afraid to take the shot, and he had done it with the calmness of a much older player. Everyone watching could see that something special was happening. This wasn't just a lucky moment—this was the beginning of something big.

After the match, Kylian was filled with pride and happiness, but he didn't let it get to his head. He thanked his teammates, listened to his coaches, and kept working hard. He knew that scoring one goal was just the start. He wanted to score many more. He wanted to help his team win, to improve his game, and to keep making his country and his family proud. His coaches praised his performance, and fans began chanting his name. People all over France started to talk about the young star from Bondy who had just scored his first professional goal.

That goal also helped Kylian gain even more confidence. Once you know you can do something, it becomes easier to try again. After scoring that goal, Kylian played with even more energy, more excitement, and more bravery. He started taking more chances, making bold runs, and trusting his instincts. Other players respected him more, and defenders had to work twice as hard to stop him. He became a key player for Monaco, helping the team reach big goals and win important matches. That first goal lit a fire inside him, a fire that never went out.

As more people around the world heard about Kylian Mbappé, they wanted to know how such a young player could be so calm, so talented, and so determined. The answer was simple—he had been preparing for this moment his entire life. Every game he had played in Bondy, every training session with his dad, every hour spent watching football videos and learning from the best—all of it led to that moment when he scored his first big goal. It wasn't just about talent. It was about heart, passion, and a belief that no dream is too big if you're willing to chase it.

In the weeks and months after that goal, Kylian continued to rise. He scored more goals, helped Monaco win the Ligue 1 title, and became one of the most talked-about young players in Europe. But no matter how many goals he scored, he always remembered that very first one. It was the goal that started it all, the one that made him realize he could play at the highest level, the one that gave him the courage to keep going.

Even today, with all the awards, trophies, and amazing moments he has experienced, Kylian often looks back at that first goal with a smile. It reminds him of how far he has come and how powerful dreams can be. He tells young players to never stop believing in themselves, to work hard, and to always be ready for their moment—because one goal, one chance, can change everything. Scoring his first big goal was the spark that lit up his path to football stardom, and it will always be a moment he treasures deep in his heart.

Chapter 8: Moving to Paris Saint-Germain

When Kylian Mbappé made the big move to Paris Saint-Germain, often called PSG, it was one of the most exciting and talked-about moments in the world of football. People all over the globe watched closely as the young superstar from Bondy took a major step in his career. Joining PSG wasn't just about switching teams—it was about returning to the city where he was born and raised, joining some of the best players in the world, and stepping onto one of the biggest stages in football. The move changed everything for Kylian and marked the beginning of a new chapter filled with challenges, dreams, and unforgettable moments.

At the time, Kylian had just completed an amazing season with AS Monaco. He had helped his team win the French league title, shocked fans with his brilliant performances in the Champions League, and become one of the most exciting young players in the world. Big clubs from all over Europe wanted to sign him. Teams from Spain, England, and Italy were watching closely. They knew Kylian had something special—he wasn't just fast and talented, he was smart, humble, and hardworking. But for Kylian, choosing PSG meant more than just playing for a top team. It meant coming home.

Paris was where Kylian's journey had started. His family lived nearby. He had trained in the parks and fields of Bondy. Now, he was being offered a chance to play for the biggest club in his home country, alongside world-famous players like Neymar. PSG promised him not only a place on the team but also a chance to grow into a global star. They believed in him, and they were ready to help him reach his full potential. Kylian and his family talked for a long time about the decision. It wasn't easy, but in the end, the idea of playing for Paris, representing the city he loved, and making his family proud was too special to pass up.

At just 18 years old, Kylian joined PSG on loan in 2017, with a plan to make the move permanent later. When the news was announced, the world went wild. Reporters filled newspapers with headlines, fans rushed to buy Mbappé jerseys, and everyone waited to see what the young star would do next. The transfer was one of the most expensive ever made for a teenager, showing just how valuable Kylian already was. But even with all the noise around him, he stayed calm and focused. He wasn't interested in being famous—he just wanted to play football, help his team, and keep improving.

Arriving at PSG was like stepping into a whole new world. The training center was huge and high-tech. The stadium, Parc des Princes, was packed with thousands of cheering fans. The locker room was filled with experienced international players. But Kylian wasn't nervous. From the first day, he worked hard, listened to the coaches, and earned the respect of his teammates. He showed that he wasn't just a young kid with potential—he was already ready to compete at the highest level.

In his very first season at PSG, Kylian made an enormous impact. He scored goal after goal, ran past defenders like they weren't even there, and played with the kind of joy and energy that made fans fall in love with him. He became part of a powerful attack alongside Neymar and Edinson Cavani, and together they formed a trio that terrified opponents. Kylian's speed, creativity, and quick thinking helped PSG win matches and trophies, and he quickly became one of the club's most important players.

But playing for PSG wasn't just about success—it also came with pressure. Everyone expected Kylian to perform in every match, score in every game, and lead the team to victory, especially in big tournaments like the Champions League. There were moments when things didn't go perfectly—games where the team lost or chances where he missed a goal. But instead of feeling discouraged, Kylian used those moments to learn and grow. He watched videos of his matches, trained even harder, and listened to feedback from his coaches. He never gave up, and that determination helped him become better with each season.

Living in Paris again also brought Kylian closer to his family. After practice or matches, he could visit his parents, talk with his younger brother Ethan, and relax in a city he had known all his life. He used his fame to support causes he cared about and to give back to his community. He donated money to charities, visited hospitals, and encouraged kids from neighborhoods like Bondy to believe in their dreams. Even though he had become a global star, he stayed connected to his roots, and people respected him for it.

Over the years, Kylian helped PSG win many trophies, including multiple Ligue 1 titles, French Cups, and Super Cups. He became the top scorer in the league several times and broke records for the number of goals scored at his age. He was named French Player of the Year more than once and earned awards for his amazing performances on the field. But one of the biggest challenges he faced at PSG was trying to help the team win the UEFA Champions League, the most important club competition in Europe.

In 2020, Kylian and PSG came closer than ever. The team reached the Champions League final for the first time in its history. Kylian played a big role in helping them get there, scoring crucial goals and creating chances for his teammates. In the final, PSG played hard, but they lost to Bayern Munich. Kylian was disappointed, but instead of giving up, he promised to come back stronger. He used that loss as motivation to keep fighting, to train harder, and to lead his team to victory in the future.

As the years went by, Kylian's leadership grew. He became a role model for younger players, both at PSG and around the world. He encouraged teamwork, respected his coaches, and always gave his best on the pitch. When the team faced tough moments, he stayed positive and kept pushing forward. When the team celebrated wins, he made sure to share the joy with everyone. He wasn't just playing for himself—he was playing for his club, his city, and his country.

Moving to PSG turned Kylian Mbappé into a household name, a symbol of hope, and a hero to millions. He became one of the most recognized athletes in the world, appearing on magazine covers, in commercials, and even in video games. But through all the fame and success, he remained focused on football, on his goals, and on inspiring others. For Kylian, joining PSG was not the end of a journey—it was the beginning of something greater. It gave him the stage he needed to show the world who he was, what he could do, and how far dreams can go when you believe in yourself and never stop working hard.

Chapter 9: Playing with Neymar and Messi

When Kylian Mbappé began playing alongside Neymar and Lionel Messi at Paris Saint-Germain (PSG), it was like a dream team come to life—three football superstars from different countries, backgrounds, and styles all wearing the same jersey and stepping onto the same field. For fans around the world, it felt like something out of a video game: one of the fastest young players in the world, one of the most skillful dribblers in history, and one of the greatest footballers of all time teaming up to create magic on the pitch. But for Kylian, playing with Neymar and Messi was more than just exciting—it was a huge opportunity to learn, grow, and take his game to even greater heights.

When Neymar joined PSG in 2017, he was already a global superstar. The Brazilian forward had made a name for himself at FC Barcelona with his fancy footwork, clever passes, and ability to score goals from almost anywhere. He was one of the most famous players in the world and known for his joyful, creative style. Kylian was only 18 when they first became teammates, and at first, he couldn't believe it. Just a few years earlier, he had watched Neymar on television, cheering for him during matches. Now, he was sharing a locker room with him, warming up beside him, and passing him the ball in real matches.

From the beginning, Neymar and Kylian built a strong connection. They communicated easily, both on and off the pitch. Neymar welcomed Kylian with kindness and respect, and Kylian responded with admiration and eagerness to learn. They often laughed during training, encouraged each other, and celebrated goals together with big smiles and high-fives. Neymar's creativity and flair blended well with Kylian's explosive speed and sharp finishing. Together, they became one of the most dangerous attacking duos in football. Defenders found it nearly impossible to stop them because they could switch positions, pass quickly, and surprise everyone with unpredictable moves.

Playing with Neymar helped Kylian understand more about teamwork and timing. Neymar didn't just dribble past players—he knew when to pass, when to slow down the game, and how to set up the perfect opportunity. Kylian paid attention to these details, adding them to his own growing skill set. He also saw how Neymar handled pressure, dealt with injuries, and stayed focused even when the whole world was watching. That kind of experience was something no training drill could teach, and Kylian soaked up every lesson.

Then in 2021, something truly incredible happened—Lionel Messi, often called the greatest football player of all time, joined PSG. Messi had spent his entire career at FC Barcelona, winning trophies, breaking records, and amazing fans with his quiet brilliance and mind-blowing talent. When it was announced that he would be joining Neymar and Mbappé in Paris, football fans everywhere were stunned. For Kylian, it was a moment of pure amazement. Messi was a legend, someone he had looked up to since he was a child. And now, they were teammates.

At first, it felt a little surreal. Kylian admitted in interviews that when Messi first walked into the PSG training center, he didn't even know how to greet him. It was like meeting a superhero. But as they started practicing together, things began to feel natural. Messi was calm, friendly, and always professional. He wasn't loud or flashy—he just let his football do the talking. And when he played, it was like watching a master artist paint a masterpiece, except with a football instead of a brush. His passes were perfectly timed, his shots were clever and controlled, and his movements were so smooth they looked like magic.

Playing with Messi taught Kylian something new—how to see the game in slow motion. Messi didn't rely on speed or strength as much as vision and intelligence. He saw spaces other players didn't, predicted what would happen before it did, and made decisions that left defenders frozen. Kylian began to combine his speed with that kind of thinking. He learned when to wait, when to sprint, when to make a clever run, and how to read Messi's cues so they could connect better during matches. Slowly, the three players—Mbappé, Neymar, and Messi—began to understand each other more and more.

Together, they became one of the most talked-about attacking trios in modern football. Fans called them "MNM," using the first letters of their last names. Whenever PSG played, the world watched closely. People wanted to see how these three stars would perform—how many goals they would score, how many amazing plays they would create, and how they would help each other shine. And they didn't disappoint. In many matches, the trio dazzled audiences with their passing, speed, and chemistry. Neymar would dribble through defenders, Messi would spot an opening, and Kylian would burst into the perfect position to score. Their teamwork made football feel like a dance.

But playing together wasn't always easy. Each player had their own style, strengths, and ideas. There were times when they had to adjust, learn how to support each other better, and put the team before personal glory. Kylian, even as the youngest of the three, showed maturity. He didn't let ego get in the way. He respected his teammates and was willing to adapt his role when needed. If Messi needed space, Kylian would move wide. If Neymar was surrounded by defenders, Kylian would drop back and offer support. The goal was always to help the team win—and to do it with joy.

Their friendship off the field also played a big role in their success. Kylian, Neymar, and Messi often shared laughs, practiced free kicks together, and supported each other during difficult times. They celebrated birthdays, joked around during warmups, and stayed close even when the media tried to create drama. That bond made them stronger during big matches and helped them trust each other when it mattered most.

With Neymar and Messi by his side, Kylian not only scored more goals—he became a more complete player. He improved his passing, his decision-making, and his leadership. He watched how Messi stayed calm under pressure and how Neymar expressed joy and creativity with every touch. These lessons helped Kylian grow not just as a footballer, but as a person. He began taking more responsibility on and off the field, speaking up as a leader, and setting an example for younger players.

Although Messi and Neymar eventually left PSG to continue their journeys elsewhere, the time Kylian spent with them left a lasting impact. He had shared the field with two of the greatest footballers of all time. He had learned from them, played alongside them, and created unforgettable memories that would stay with him forever. He had faced challenges, won trophies, and grown into a true star—someone others now looked up to, just as he had once looked up to them.

Playing with Neymar and Messi was more than just about goals and games. It was about friendship, learning, growth, and sharing the joy of football at the highest level. For Kylian Mbappé, it was an unforgettable chapter in his incredible story—a time when he played with legends, became one himself, and proved that even dreams that seem too big can come true when you believe in your talent and play with your heart.

Chapter 10: Winning the World Cup at Nineteen

When Kylian Mbappé won the FIFA World Cup at just nineteen years old, he didn't just make headlines—he made history. It was one of those rare moments in sports when something magical happens that the whole world remembers forever. For most football players, winning the World Cup is the biggest dream of all, something they hope for after many years of playing. But Kylian did it before he even turned twenty, becoming one of the youngest players ever to lift the trophy. What made it even more special was the way he played during the tournament—fast, fearless, full of energy, and with the confidence of a seasoned professional. The world watched as this teenager helped lead the French national team to victory, showing that age doesn't matter when you have heart, talent, and the courage to chase your dreams.

The journey to the 2018 World Cup in Russia started long before the tournament began. Kylian had already impressed football fans with his amazing performances at AS Monaco and Paris Saint-Germain. His speed, skill, and goal-scoring ability had made him one of the most exciting young players in the world. So, when the French national team manager, Didier Deschamps, selected him to represent France, it didn't surprise many people—but it still felt incredible. Kylian was going to wear the blue jersey of his country, play on the biggest stage of all, and try to help his team win the most important tournament in football.

Even before the tournament kicked off, Kylian knew what an honor it was to represent France. He had grown up watching old videos of World Cup matches, dreaming of one day playing in them himself. Now, the time had come. He trained hard, listened carefully to his coaches, and stayed focused. He wasn't there to just be a young star—he wanted to help his team win. The pressure was huge, with millions of fans watching, reporters asking questions, and opponents trying to stop him. But Kylian didn't let the pressure get to him. Instead, he used it as motivation to give his best every time he stepped on the pitch.

In the early matches of the tournament, Kylian played with energy and confidence. He didn't act like a nervous teenager—he acted like a leader. He made smart passes, created chances for his teammates, and used his incredible speed to break through defenses. He quickly caught the world's attention, especially in the Round of 16 match against Argentina. In that game, Kylian showed just how unstoppable he could be. He scored two amazing goals and helped win a penalty by sprinting across the field so fast that defenders couldn't catch him. That performance shocked everyone. Fans all over the world started talking about the young French star who had just outplayed some of the best players in the world.

After that match, Kylian became a global sensation. Newspapers called him a "wonderkid," TV shows replayed his goals over and over, and people from every country began cheering for him. But Kylian stayed humble. He didn't brag or act like he was better than anyone else. He kept working hard, kept supporting his teammates, and kept focusing on the next match. In the quarterfinal and semifinal games, he continued to play brilliantly, helping France move closer and closer to the final.

Then came the big day—the 2018 FIFA World Cup Final. France would play against Croatia in front of millions of fans around the globe. The stadium in Moscow was full of excitement, and the tension was high. Everyone knew this match would decide which team would be crowned world champions. Kylian, still only nineteen, stepped onto the field with a calm expression. He was ready. He knew this was the biggest match of his life so far, but he didn't let fear or nerves take over. Instead, he played with the same joy and focus he had always shown, from his early days in Bondy to his big nights with PSG.

During the final, Kylian once again showed why he was so special. He ran fearlessly at defenders, passed the ball with precision, and always stayed one step ahead of the game. And then, in the 65th minute, he scored a goal—a brilliant shot from outside the box that flew past the goalkeeper. It was France's fourth goal of the match, and it helped seal their 4–2 victory over Croatia. With that goal, Kylian became only the second teenager in history to score in a World Cup Final, after the legendary Pelé did it in 1958. Pelé himself later praised Kylian, calling him a star and welcoming him to a very special club. It was a moment of pure magic.

When the final whistle blew and France was declared the World Cup champion, Kylian dropped to his knees, overwhelmed with emotion. All the hard work, the long hours of training, the sacrifices he and his family had made—it had all led to this. His teammates rushed to hug him, and together they lifted the golden trophy high into the air. The crowd roared, confetti filled the stadium, and the players danced and cheered with pure joy. It was a dream come true—not just for Kylian, but for all of France.

After the match, Kylian was awarded the FIFA World Cup Best Young Player award, given to the most outstanding young footballer in the tournament. He had scored four goals, made countless plays, and shown maturity far beyond his years. He had helped lead his country to glory and inspired millions of young fans around the world. People everywhere celebrated not just the victory, but the rise of a new football hero.

But even after winning the World Cup, Kylian didn't stop working. He didn't act like he had already done everything. Instead, he said that winning the trophy made him want to do even more. He wanted to keep improving, keep helping his team, and keep making his country proud. He donated his entire World Cup salary—around half a million dollars—to a children's charity, showing that he cared about giving back and helping others. That act of kindness made fans love him even more. He wasn't just a great player—he was a great person.

Winning the World Cup at nineteen didn't just make Kylian Mbappé a champion. It made him a symbol of hope, hard work, and what's possible when you believe in your dreams. He showed the world that age doesn't matter when you have courage, talent, and determination. He inspired kids everywhere to chase their goals, to never give up, and to always play with joy and passion. For Kylian, lifting that golden trophy wasn't the end—it was just the beginning of a long, exciting journey. And it was a moment that will live in football history forever.

Chapter 11: Facing Tough Challenges

Even though Kylian Mbappé is one of the most talented and famous footballers in the world, his journey hasn't always been easy. Just like any great hero, he has had to face many tough challenges—moments that tested his strength, patience, and determination. These challenges didn't stop him. Instead, they helped him grow, learn more about himself, and become even stronger. Behind all the goals, trophies, and cheering fans, there are stories of hard days, big decisions, and moments of doubt. Facing tough challenges is a part of every great player's story, and Kylian's is no different.

One of the first big challenges Kylian had to deal with was pressure. From a young age, people were watching him closely. Scouts, coaches, and football fans saw his talent early on and expected him to do great things. That might sound exciting, but it can also be very stressful, especially for a teenager. Imagine being only 16 or 17 and already being called "the next big star." Every time he stepped onto the field, people expected him to be amazing. If he played well, people cheered. But if he made a mistake, everyone noticed. That kind of attention can be really hard to handle, but Kylian didn't let it crush him. Instead, he focused on working hard, listening to his coaches, and trying to improve a little every day.

Another challenge he faced was dealing with criticism. No matter how good a player is, there will always be people who say mean things. Sometimes it's reporters in newspapers or fans on social media who say he should have passed instead of shooting, or that he didn't play well in a big game. After France lost the Euro 2020 tournament and Kylian missed a penalty in a shootout, some people unfairly blamed him. Some fans even sent him hurtful messages. That was a really tough time for him. He had tried his best, but football can be unpredictable, and sometimes things just don't go your way. Instead of hiding or giving up, Kylian stayed strong. He apologized to the fans, supported his teammates, and promised to come back stronger. He showed courage and maturity even when others weren't kind.

Injuries have also been part of Kylian's challenges. As a fast and skillful player, he often gets tackled hard by defenders trying to stop him. There have been games where he limped off the field or had to rest for weeks to heal. Injuries can be very frustrating, especially for someone who loves playing as much as Kylian does. Being told you can't train or play, even for a little while, can feel like a punishment. But Kylian used those moments to rest, recover, and come back even better. He followed his doctors' advice, stayed patient, and worked hard during recovery to regain his strength. Those quiet, behind-the-scenes moments—doing exercises alone in the gym, watching games from the sidelines—are not as exciting as scoring goals, but they are just as important.

Sometimes, the challenges were about big decisions. One of the biggest choices Kylian had to make was whether to stay at Paris Saint-Germain or move to another giant club like Real Madrid. Both teams wanted him, and millions of fans around the world waited to see what he would choose. People gave him advice, rumors spread, and newspapers wrote story after story. That kind of decision isn't simple. It involves thinking about your family, your future, your happiness, and your goals. In the end, Kylian decided to stay in Paris for a while longer, choosing to help his hometown club chase new dreams. It showed that he wasn't just thinking about money or fame—he wanted to grow as a leader and make a difference.

Another tough challenge came during the World Cup final in 2022. France was playing against Argentina in one of the most dramatic matches in World Cup history. At first, things didn't go well for France. They were losing, and the team was struggling. But Kylian didn't give up. He scored a hat-trick—three incredible goals—and brought his team back into the game. Even though France lost in the penalty shootout, Kylian had given everything he had. He was sad about the loss, but he held his head high. He had shown the world what a true champion looks like—not just someone who wins, but someone who fights with heart, never gives up, and respects the game.

Off the field, Kylian has also faced the challenge of growing up in front of the world. Most teenagers get to make mistakes in private, but Kylian has lived much of his life in the spotlight. Every word he says, every picture he takes, every move he makes is watched by millions. He has had to learn how to handle fame, stay grounded, and protect his privacy. He has talked about how important his family is in helping him stay focused. They remind him of where he came from and what really matters. Even though he's a superstar, he's also just a young man who likes playing video games, laughing with friends, and spending time with loved ones.

Through all these challenges, Kylian has stayed true to himself. He's not perfect—no one is—but he keeps learning, growing, and trying to be better. He doesn't hide from difficulties. He faces them head-on, with strength and a positive attitude. He listens, adapts, and keeps moving forward. That's what makes him a true role model. Not just because he's fast or scores amazing goals, but because he shows young people that it's okay to struggle, to make mistakes, and to have bad days—as long as you keep trying, keep believing, and keep being kind.

Facing tough challenges has shaped Kylian into the person and player he is today. Each difficult moment has made him stronger, wiser, and more determined. He knows that success doesn't come easily. It takes effort, sacrifice, and the courage to stand up when things go wrong. And every time he steps back onto the field, with a smile on his face and fire in his heart, he reminds the world that challenges don't stop you—they make you unstoppable.

Chapter 12: The Heart of a Team Player

Kylian Mbappé may be known around the world for his incredible speed, dazzling footwork, and jaw-dropping goals, but what makes him truly special isn't just what he does with the ball—it's the way he plays with his heart. Deep down, Mbappé isn't just a superstar chasing trophies or records. He's someone who understands the power of teamwork, the value of lifting others up, and the importance of being there for his teammates in every moment, whether the team is winning or losing. Being the heart of a team player means thinking beyond yourself. It means passing when you could score, cheering when others shine, and standing tall when things don't go your way. Mbappé has shown over and over again that he's not just a solo star—he's a team-first player who plays with courage, kindness, and a strong spirit of unity.

From the time he was a young boy playing on the fields of Bondy, Kylian was taught that football was a team game. His father, who coached him from the beginning, made sure he understood that no one wins a match alone. Kylian learned to pass, to move into space, and to celebrate not only his goals but also the goals his teammates scored. Even then, he wasn't just focused on being the best—he wanted the whole team to grow. He listened carefully during training, encouraged the other kids, and celebrated every small improvement. These habits stayed with him as he grew older and moved onto bigger teams with bigger dreams.

When he joined AS Monaco as a teenager, he showed that same team spirit. Even though he was often the youngest player on the field, he didn't let that stop him from playing with confidence—but he also didn't let success get to his head. He treated his older teammates with respect and learned from them every day. He understood that they had more experience, and he wanted to be part of a team that worked together like a family. He played with joy and shared that joy freely.

When someone else scored, he was the first to hug them. When a teammate was injured or disappointed, he gave them a pat on the back or a few words of encouragement. These small actions helped build a strong team spirit.

At Paris Saint-Germain, where he plays with some of the biggest football names in the world, Kylian has continued to show what being a team player really means. He has played beside legends like Neymar and Lionel Messi, both of whom have huge fan bases and long lists of achievements. But instead of trying to outshine them, Kylian has always tried to connect with them—to learn, to support, and to share the spotlight. He passes the ball when it makes sense, even if he could go for goal himself. He doesn't just want to score—he wants his team to win, and he wants his teammates to feel proud too.

One thing that sets Kylian apart is how he treats younger or less experienced players. He remembers what it felt like to be the new kid, to be nervous before a big match, or to worry about making a mistake. That's why he goes out of his way to help others feel confident. Whether it's offering advice, sharing a joke in the locker room, or sticking up for someone who's struggling, Kylian plays the role of a big brother to many of his teammates. He believes that when everyone feels supported and included, the team becomes stronger.

He also knows how important it is to listen and learn. Even though he's famous and has achieved so much, he doesn't act like he knows everything. He listens to his coaches, takes their advice seriously, and follows the game plan. He understands that football is not just about individual brilliance—it's about working together, staying organized, and trusting each other. When he wears the captain's armband, he does so with humility. He knows that being a leader doesn't mean shouting the loudest. It means leading by example, staying calm under pressure, and showing others that you believe in them.

Mbappé's team-first attitude shines through when the stakes are high. In big matches, like World Cup games or Champions League finals, the pressure is enormous. Everyone wants to be the hero. But Kylian always plays for the team. He defends when needed, helps organize the attack, and encourages his teammates to keep fighting. In the 2018 World Cup, even though he scored important goals and won awards, he was always quick to share credit with others. He thanked his teammates and praised their efforts. He never made it all about himself, even though the world was cheering his name.

In tough times, too, Kylian stays loyal to his teammates. After France lost the Euro 2020 tournament, he was heartbroken, especially because he missed a crucial penalty. But instead of blaming others or hiding from the media, he stood tall and took responsibility. He thanked his teammates for their support and reminded fans that football is a team sport. His strength and honesty during that difficult moment inspired many people and showed just how much he cares about those around him.

Off the field, Kylian continues to act like a team player. He speaks kindly about other athletes, supports causes that help children and families, and always talks about football as something that brings people together. He doesn't just want to win trophies—he wants to make a positive difference. He understands that being part of a team is not just about scoring goals. It's about being there for others, building friendships, and creating moments that everyone can be proud of.

Sometimes, being a team player means making sacrifices. There have been moments when Kylian had to give up personal glory for the good of the team. Whether it was playing out of position, following a coach's strategy, or helping a struggling teammate, Kylian always put the team's needs first. And even when people talked about him in the media—guessing if he was happy or what his next move might be—he stayed focused on his job: helping his teammates, working hard, and playing with heart.

Being the heart of a team player means more than just wearing a jersey. It means showing up every day with a smile, sharing your strengths, supporting your teammates, and believing in something bigger than yourself. Kylian Mbappé is proof that even the brightest stars can shine in a team—and that when you play with love, courage, and respect, you don't just win games. You win hearts. His story reminds young players everywhere that greatness isn't just about talent—it's about teamwork, attitude, and giving your all for the people beside you.

Chapter 13: Helping Kids Around the World

Kylian Mbappé is not just a football superstar—he's also a kind, caring, and generous person who believes in using his success to make the world a better place. While millions of people know him for his lightning-fast runs and unforgettable goals, there's another side to him that's just as powerful: his big heart. He never forgot what it was like to grow up in a regular neighborhood, where not everything was easy, and he has always wanted to help children who face struggles in life. Whether they're sick, poor, or just need a bit of hope, Kylian tries to be there for them. Helping kids around the world has become one of the most important parts of his life, and he does it with the same passion and energy that he brings to the football pitch.

From the very beginning of his career, even when he was still a teenager, Kylian made it clear that he wanted to give back. He didn't want to just earn fame and money for himself—he wanted to share it, especially with children. After France won the FIFA World Cup in 2018 and Kylian became an international hero, he made a surprising and generous choice: he donated all of the money he earned during the tournament to a charity that helps children with disabilities and illnesses. That's right—every single euro. For most people, that much money would be a big deal, but Kylian said that he didn't play football for money. He played because he loved it, and he wanted to use his success to do something meaningful.

The charity he supported is called "Premiers de Cordée," a French organization that brings sports to children in hospitals. These are kids who are going through hard times, battling serious illnesses, and sometimes stuck in their hospital rooms for weeks or months. The charity organizes fun sports days, games, and visits from famous athletes to cheer them up. Kylian has personally visited some of these children. He plays games with them, takes pictures, signs shirts, and most importantly, listens to them. He doesn't rush through these visits or treat them like a job. He takes his time, makes each child feel special, and gives them a reason to smile. For many of these kids, meeting Mbappé isn't just exciting—it's a moment they'll remember forever.

But Kylian didn't stop there. He wanted to do more. So, in 2020, he launched his very own charity called "Inspired by KM." This organization is focused on helping kids reach their full potential, no matter where they come from. It supports children in many ways—helping them with education, giving them access to sports, providing resources for their dreams, and reminding them that they matter. One of the goals of the charity is to help children believe in themselves, just like Kylian believed in himself when he was a kid in Bondy with a big dream.

"Inspired by KM" works with schools and community programs. It helps kids who might not have many opportunities by giving them what they need to succeed—books, supplies, coaching, even meals or transportation. Sometimes, all a child needs is someone to say, "I believe in you." And that's exactly what Kylian's charity is all about. It says to kids all over the world, "You're not alone. You can dream big, and there are people here to help you."

Mbappé also speaks out about things that matter, especially when it comes to children's futures. He talks about education, health, and fairness. He knows that not every child gets the same start in life, and he wants to change that. He has supported campaigns that fight racism, bullying, and poverty. He believes that every child, no matter where they're born or what they look like, deserves to be treated with respect and love. In interviews and speeches, he reminds the world that helping children is not something extra—it's something necessary.

During the COVID 19 pandemic, Kylian stepped up again. He donated money to charities that were helping children and families who had lost jobs or didn't have enough to eat. He made sure people had what they needed to stay safe and healthy. He also helped raise awareness by using his voice to encourage people to care for one another. He reminded everyone that even small actions—like washing hands, wearing a mask, or helping a neighbor—can make a big difference. In times of crisis, he showed what it means to be a true role model.

Around the world, Kylian's kindness has inspired other young people to get involved too. Some kids have started their own small projects—collecting toys for hospitals, raising money for schools, or volunteering in their neighborhoods—all because they saw what Mbappé was doing and wanted to follow his example. That's the amazing thing about kindness—it spreads. One good action leads to another, and before long, there's a whole wave of goodness touching lives everywhere.

Mbappé's caring nature also shines through in how he talks to young fans. Whether it's signing autographs after a game, stopping to take a selfie, or responding to letters from kids who look up to him, he always tries to make time. And it's not just for kids who are strong or healthy—it's especially for those who are sick, shy, or struggling. He sees their bravery and wants to lift them up. He knows that sometimes, even just a smile or a kind word can change a bad day into a good one.

And while he does all of this with great generosity, he doesn't do it for attention. He doesn't post every visit or donation on social media. Often, he helps quietly, behind the scenes, because it's not about getting praise—it's about doing what's right. His family taught him to be humble, to care for others, and to always stay grounded, no matter how famous he becomes. That's why people trust him. That's why kids believe him. He doesn't just say he cares—he shows it, time and time again.

Helping kids around the world isn't just a hobby for Kylian Mbappé—it's a mission. Whether he's scoring goals on the pitch or changing lives off of it, he brings the same passion, effort, and love.

He proves that being a hero isn't about being the fastest or strongest. It's about having a heart that's big enough to help others, especially those who need it most. And that's exactly what Kylian does, every single day. For kids everywhere, he's not just a football champion—he's a champion of kindness, hope, and dreams.

Chapter 14: Breaking Records Fast

Kylian Mbappé has amazed the world with his unbelievable speed—not just the way he sprints across the football field like a flash of lightning, but also how quickly he has broken some of football's biggest records. Most players spend many years trying to make history, but Kylian did it faster than almost anyone before him. From the moment he started his professional career, people could see he was different. It wasn't just that he was fast with his feet—it was that he was fast at reaching milestones, fast at scoring goals, and fast at rising to the top of the football world. Breaking records fast became something that Kylian Mbappé did again and again, and each time, he proved that age is just a number when you have talent, drive, and a fearless heart.

It all started when he was still a teenager playing for AS Monaco. At just 16 years old, Kylian made his first appearance for the club's senior team, and he didn't just stand on the field—he made an impact. He became the youngest player ever to debut for Monaco, breaking a record previously held by none other than Thierry Henry, one of France's most legendary footballers. That was the first sign that Kylian was going to do big things—and do them quickly. Not long after, he also became Monaco's youngest-ever goal scorer. The crowd cheered as the young boy with quick feet and bright eyes celebrated, not realizing he was just getting started.

Soon, Mbappé was scoring goals almost every week, helping Monaco win the French Ligue 1 title for the first time in 17 years. He did things most players only dream of—and he was still in his teens. He scored in the UEFA Champions League, the top football competition in Europe, becoming one of the youngest players to ever score in that tournament. He was fearless against teams with older, more experienced players, and his name started spreading across Europe like wildfire. Fans, coaches, and football legends couldn't believe how someone so young was already playing like a star.

Then came his move to Paris Saint-Germain, and with it, even more chances to break records. He became one of the most expensive teenagers in football history when PSG signed him, showing just how much people believed in him. And he didn't disappoint. In one season after another, Kylian broke records for most goals scored by a player under 20, the fastest to reach 10 goals in Ligue 1, and the youngest French player to score in the Champions League knockout stage. He was setting new milestones at lightning speed.

One of the most exciting records he broke came during the 2018 FIFA World Cup. At only 19 years old, Kylian became the youngest French player to score in a World Cup. And that wasn't all—he went on to score in the final, becoming only the second teenager ever to do that. The first was Pelé, the Brazilian legend who scored in the 1958 final. When Pelé heard about Mbappé's achievement, he congratulated him and even joked that he might have to come out of retirement! That moment wasn't just about breaking a record—it was about joining a small group of football greats who changed the game at a young age.

Mbappé's pace on the field also helped him set records for sprinting. In one match, he ran so fast that people compared his speed to Olympic runners. At his top speed, he reached over 38 kilometers per hour (about 23.6 miles per hour), faster than most defenders could even imagine. Sports scientists, coaches, and fans were stunned. They called him a "human rocket" and said defenders couldn't catch him even if they tried. His quick runs weren't just exciting to watch—they led to goals, assists, and game-winning moments.

As he continued to play for PSG, the records kept coming. He became the youngest player to reach 100 goals for the club. He also became the fastest player to reach certain goal totals in French football history. Every time he stepped onto the field, it seemed like he had a chance to set another record. Newspapers started printing lists of all the records he had broken, and commentators couldn't keep up with how quickly his achievements were stacking up. One day it would be "youngest to score 20 Champions League goals," the next it would be "most goals in a calendar year for PSG." And through it all, Kylian stayed focused and humble.

Even when facing tough competition in the UEFA Champions League, Kylian rose to the occasion. Against Barcelona in 2021, he scored a stunning hat trick in the round of 16—the first time anyone had done that against Barcelona in a knockout game since the tournament began. People around the world cheered, and headlines everywhere read: "Mbappé Makes History." He wasn't just breaking records in France anymore—he was making his mark across Europe and beyond.

Then came the 2022 World Cup in Qatar, and with it, even more chances to break records. Mbappé scored eight goals in the tournament, more than any other player, and he won the Golden Boot award. In the final against Argentina, when France was struggling, he scored three goals—an incredibly rare World Cup final hat trick. Even though France lost the match in a dramatic penalty shootout, Mbappé's performance was one of the greatest in football history. He became the first player since 1966 to score three goals in a World Cup final. That night, even in defeat, he was a winner in the eyes of the world.

As of now, Mbappé has become PSG's all-time top scorer, breaking a record held by Edinson Cavani, another legendary striker. He achieved this in fewer games and at a younger age than anyone expected. His goal-scoring ability, his quick thinking, and his love for the game helped him reach the top fast. He's also been the top scorer in Ligue 1 multiple seasons in a row, something very few players have done.

But what's really amazing is that Kylian never lets the records go to his head. He celebrates the milestones, of course, but he always says the most important thing is helping the team win. He doesn't chase personal records just to be the best—he works hard, trains every day, and plays with all his heart because he loves football. And that love is what powers everything he does.

Breaking records fast isn't easy. It takes discipline, passion, and a lot of sacrifice. Kylian trains even when he's tired. He studies games, eats healthy, and sleeps well so he can always be ready. He listens to his coaches, supports his teammates, and keeps learning. He knows that talent alone isn't enough—you have to respect the game and keep giving it your all. That's why he keeps climbing higher and higher, and why fans believe that many more records will fall as long as Kylian Mbappé is on the pitch.

His story shows kids everywhere that it's possible to do amazing things at a young age if you work hard, believe in yourself, and stay focused. Whether it's breaking a goal record, running faster than anyone else, or scoring in a World Cup final, Kylian proves that dreams really can come true—and they might come true faster than you think.

Chapter 15: Life Off the Field

When Kylian Mbappé isn't dazzling crowds in stadiums, scoring goals, or lifting trophies, he lives a life that's full of meaning, balance, and quiet strength. While many people see only his fast runs, clever passes, and highlight-reel goals, there's another side of him that's just as important: the person he is off the field. Life off the field is where he relaxes, reflects, connects with family and friends, gives back to the world, and stays grounded in who he truly is. It's where Kylian Mbappé isn't just a football star—he's a thoughtful young man, a role model, a son, a friend, and a dreamer with a big heart and big hopes for others.

Even though Kylian is famous all around the world, he still lives a life that is filled with simple joys. One of the most important parts of his life off the field is his family. He is very close to his parents and his younger brother, Ethan. His father, Wilfried, helped coach him when he was a child and played a big role in his development as both a player and a person. His mother, Fayza, once a handball player herself, has always supported him and reminded him to stay true to himself. They've been there for him through the highs and lows, cheering him on from the sidelines and guiding him when things get tough. Kylian often says that his family is his foundation—the people who helped shape his character and remind him of what truly matters.

He also has a strong bond with his little brother, Ethan, who dreams of following in Kylian's footsteps. The two share a close relationship filled with laughter, games, and encouragement. When Kylian has free time, he loves spending it with Ethan, whether it's watching movies, playing video games, or just relaxing together at home. He's not just a big brother—he's also a mentor, helping Ethan believe in his own path and reminding him that success takes time, effort, and kindness.

Kylian's life off the field also includes things that many kids love—he enjoys video games like FIFA and other sports games, and sometimes even plays as himself in the game, just for fun. He likes listening to music, especially rap and R&B, and often uses music to get into the right mood before matches or unwind after a long day. He's a fan of pop culture, movies, and art, and he's interested in learning about different parts of the world. Even though he's very famous, Kylian tries to keep his personal time peaceful. He doesn't go out to flashy parties or big events all the time. He prefers to spend his free moments doing things that make him feel happy, healthy, and calm.

Another important part of Kylian's life off the field is his love for helping others. He believes that being a role model comes with responsibility. He doesn't just want to be admired for his football skills—he wants to make a difference in people's lives. Through his charity work, especially with his foundation "Inspired by KM," he supports children who face challenges. Whether it's providing school supplies, sports equipment, mentorship, or just a listening ear, Kylian shows that even a few kind actions can have a big impact. He often says that when you are given a lot in life, it's important to give something back. That's why he spends time visiting hospitals, meeting kids, and offering hope to those who need it most.

Kylian is also someone who takes his health seriously. To perform at such a high level on the pitch, he has to stay in top shape. That means eating nutritious meals, getting enough sleep, and taking care of his body. But it also means taking care of his mind. He understands the importance of rest and mental health, especially with the pressures of being a world-famous athlete. Sometimes, he takes quiet walks, reads, or talks with close friends to stay centered. These quiet moments help him reset and return to the field with energy and focus.

Even with all his fame, Kylian never acts like he's better than others. He treats fans, teammates, coaches, and strangers with respect. He is polite in interviews, thoughtful in public speeches, and kind when people ask for autographs or selfies. He knows that being humble is just as important as being talented. People often say that he has "the feet of a champion and the heart of a gentleman." That's why fans of all ages look up to him—not just because of what he does, but because of who he is.

Kylian also uses his voice to stand up for important causes. He has spoken out against racism, bullying, and unfair treatment in sports. He believes in equality and inclusion, and he wants every child to feel proud of who they are. He once said that football belongs to everyone, no matter where they come from or what they look like. When Kylian speaks, people listen—not just because he's famous, but because he speaks from the heart.

When it comes to personal goals, Kylian dreams big but stays focused. Off the field, he has shown interest in business, fashion, and possibly even filmmaking in the future. He wants to explore the world beyond football and use his creativity to inspire people in new ways. But he never rushes—he knows that each part of life deserves attention and care. He takes his time, learns from mentors, and keeps imagining what's possible.

Sometimes, his off-the-field life can be difficult too. Being famous means having cameras follow you, hearing rumors, and dealing with pressure every day. Kylian handles all of this with grace. He doesn't let gossip distract him or let success change him. Instead, he remembers where he came from, listens to those he trusts, and keeps his feet firmly on the ground. That's why people say Kylian has an "old soul"—even though he's young, he carries himself with wisdom and strength.

Life off the field is where Kylian refuels his spirit. It's where he laughs with his brother, talks to his parents, plays games, reads books, helps others, and dreams new dreams. It's the part of his life that keeps him balanced, joyful, and ready to give his best every time he steps onto the pitch. For Kylian Mbappé, football is a huge part of his life, but it's not the only part. What makes him truly remarkable is that, even with all the noise and fame, he never forgets to be kind, thoughtful, and human.

So, whether he's wearing a football jersey, a hoodie at home, or a suit at a charity event, Kylian Mbappé shows the world what it means to live with purpose and heart. He reminds us all that being a champion is about more than scoring goals—it's about how you treat people, what you believe in, and how you choose to live each day, both on the field and off it.

Chapter 16: Fans Around the Globe

All around the world, from small villages to giant cities, from icy mountains to sunny beaches, there are kids, teens, and even grown-ups who know the name Kylian Mbappé. His talent, smile, and incredible story have made him a hero far beyond the football pitch. Everywhere he goes, fans wave flags, hold signs, wear his jersey, and shout his name with excitement. They feel connected to him—not just because he scores amazing goals, but because he's a player who inspires them, someone they can look up to. Kylian Mbappé has fans around the globe, and each of them has their own reason for loving and cheering for him. Some admire his speed, others love his teamwork, and many admire the kindness and respect he shows both on and off the field.

In his home country of France, Mbappé is more than just a footballer—he's a national treasure. When he plays in the blue jersey of the French national team, people from every region, city, and neighborhood come together to support him. Young children wear his number 10 jersey with pride. Bakeries hang his picture in their windows. Schools have sports days where kids pretend to be Mbappé, racing across fields and copying his goal celebrations. Even people who don't usually watch football will tune in when he's playing. After France won the World Cup in 2018, millions of people poured into the streets, waving the French flag and chanting his name. In that moment, Kylian became a symbol of hope and unity—a young man from a neighborhood called Bondy who showed the world that anything is possible.

But Mbappé's fan base doesn't stop at France's borders. In Spain, Germany, Italy, and the United Kingdom, football fans talk about him with excitement and admiration. In Brazil and Argentina, countries known for producing their own football legends, young players look up to Mbappé and try to match his speed and style. In Africa, especially in places like Cameroon and Algeria where Kylian's family has roots, he is loved not just for his football but for what he represents—strength, pride, and connection to his heritage. Kids in villages with only one soccer ball take turns pretending to be Mbappé. They dream of one day making their own mark on the game, just like he did.

In Asia, Mbappé is a massive star. From Japan to India, from China to South Korea, football fans follow his matches closely. On social media, they share videos of his goals, cheer his victories, and support him after tough games. Many of them stay up late into the night or wake up early in the morning just to watch him play live. In schools, his posters are hung on classroom walls. In football academies, coaches use videos of him to teach kids how to move, pass, and think like a great player. He has visited countries across Asia, and each time, the crowds have welcomed him with cheers, flowers, and endless joy.

In the United States and Canada, where soccer is still growing in popularity, Mbappé has become one of the most recognized faces of the sport. Kids playing in weekend leagues know his name. They copy his signature celebrations and practice shooting with their right foot just like him. In big cities like New York, Los Angeles, and Toronto, stores sell his jerseys, and giant screens show his matches. He has appeared in interviews, commercials, and even video games, becoming a global face for football's bright future. American athletes from other sports—like basketball and American football—have praised his talent, showing how his influence goes beyond just one sport.

In Australia, football fans have a deep respect for Mbappé's abilities and his character. Even though the time difference means games often happen early in the morning or late at night, fans wake up and gather to watch him. They organize fan clubs, write articles, and cheer him on from the other side of the world. His international appeal proves that football truly is a global language, and that great talent and kindness can connect people across oceans and continents.

One reason fans around the globe admire Mbappé so much is that he's more than just a great athlete—he's also a great human being.

After matches, he doesn't just celebrate his own success. He thanks his teammates, shakes hands with opponents, and often gives his shirt to a young fan in the crowd. These small moments make a big difference. They show that he sees his fans not as just people watching from afar, but as a community that supports and motivates him. He never forgets that it's the fans who make the sport special, and he treats them with respect and appreciation.

Social media has also helped Kylian connect with his fans everywhere. He shares photos, messages, and videos, giving a glimpse into his life. Whether he's showing a funny moment in training, posting about a charity project, or encouraging kids to chase their dreams, he always sends a message of positivity and hope. Fans reply with love, drawings, poems, and thank-you messages. Some even create music or art inspired by him. The bond between Kylian and his fans is strong, and it keeps growing.

Mbappé's influence is especially powerful among young fans. Children of all ages see him as proof that you don't have to be perfect or come from a rich background to succeed. He talks openly about his journey, including the challenges, hard work, and the people who helped him. This honesty makes fans feel closer to him. He inspires them to keep going, even when life is hard, because they know that he once had to work just as hard to get where he is now. For many young people, seeing Kylian Mbappé succeed gives them the courage to believe in themselves.

Even in countries where football isn't the most popular sport, Mbappé's name is still known. People may not watch every match, but they know he's someone special. They've seen his highlights, read about his kindness, or heard how he donated his World Cup earnings to help sick children. Stories like these travel far and fast, and they help build a fanbase that's built not only on his skills but also on his goodness.

Kylian never takes his fans for granted. He often says that their love gives him strength. Before big games, he sometimes looks at the messages and drawings sent by fans to remind himself why he plays. When fans sing his name or wave his jersey, he smiles with pride and gratitude. He knows that fame is temporary, but love and connection are forever. That's why he always makes time to wave, sign autographs, and share a kind word—even when he's tired or rushing to the next event.

From stadiums packed with thousands to small towns with one television, fans everywhere cheer for Kylian Mbappé. They sing his name in many languages. They write it on their notebooks, paint it on walls, and dream of meeting him one day. He's not just a footballer—he's a global inspiration. And through his journey, he brings the world a little closer together, one fan at a time.

So, whether it's a young boy kicking a ball in Nigeria, a girl practicing in Tokyo, a family cheering in Brazil, or a student writing a letter in Canada, the love for Kylian Mbappé stretches across every continent. His fans aren't just watching—they're believing, learning, and dreaming alongside him. And that might be the greatest victory of all.

Chapter 17: Staying Humble and Focused

Even though Kylian Mbappé has become one of the most famous football players in the world, with crowds cheering his name, cameras flashing wherever he goes, and headlines calling him a superstar, he has always stayed humble and focused. That means he never lets success go to his head, and he always remembers what's truly important—working hard, helping others, being kind, and never forgetting where he came from. Staying humble is not easy when you're famous, and staying focused is even harder when there are so many distractions. But Kylian has learned how to stay grounded and keep his eyes on what matters most, both on and off the field.

From the time he was a little boy in Bondy, a neighborhood just outside Paris, Kylian was taught to treat everyone with respect. His parents, who have always played a big part in his life, told him that being talented was a gift, but being humble was a choice. His father coached him in football, but he also taught him lessons about character, reminding him that a true champion is someone who never looks down on others. His mother showed him how to stay strong and fair, and how to keep believing in himself without becoming arrogant. These early lessons stayed with Kylian as he rose through the ranks of football, from local pitches to world-famous stadiums.

Even when he was still a teenager playing for AS Monaco, people started comparing him to legends like Pelé and Thierry Henry. Reporters followed his every move. Fans waited outside to catch a glimpse of him. He was breaking records, scoring goals, and making football history at a very young age. But instead of showing off or bragging, Kylian always kept his feet on the ground. In interviews, he thanked his teammates, gave credit to his coaches, and talked about how much he still had to learn. He didn't pretend to be perfect. He just kept training, listening, and growing.

When he joined Paris Saint-Germain and began playing alongside famous stars like Neymar and Lionel Messi, he could have let all the attention make him act like a big shot. But he didn't. He respected his teammates, worked hard in practice, and showed that he wanted to be part of a team—not just a star on his own. He knew that one player doesn't win games by himself. It takes everyone working together. Kylian helped build strong friendships with his teammates, passed the ball when needed, and always played with heart. Even when people called him the best, he said there was still room to improve.

One of the things that helps Kylian stay humble is his connection to his roots. He often visits his old neighborhood in Bondy and talks with kids who have big dreams like he once did. He reminds them that no matter how far you go, it's important to remember where you started. He gives back to his community through his charity work, helping children who face tough situations. He donates money, visits hospitals, and creates programs that give young people a chance to succeed. He doesn't do these things for praise—he does them because he truly cares.

Staying focused is just as important to Kylian as staying humble. With so much going on—games, interviews, travel, social media, and public events—it would be easy to get distracted. But Kylian knows that if he wants to stay at the top of his game, he has to stay locked in. That means practicing every day, eating healthy, getting enough sleep, and always looking for ways to get better. He watches replays of his matches to see what he could improve. He listens to advice from his coaches. He works on his fitness and keeps training hard, even when he's already one of the best.

There have been moments in his career when things didn't go perfectly. Like when he missed a penalty during the Euro 2020 tournament or when France lost the World Cup final in 2022, even after he scored three incredible goals. In those moments, Kylian could have gotten upset, blamed others, or walked away. But instead, he took responsibility, learned from the experience, and promised to come back stronger. He didn't let failure shake him. He stayed focused on the next goal, the next game, and the next opportunity to grow.

Even off the pitch, Kylian keeps a simple and balanced life. He doesn't spend all his time at parties or chasing fame. Instead, he enjoys quiet time with his family, plays video games with his younger brother, reads books, and listens to music. These moments help him relax and stay calm. They remind him that happiness doesn't come from being in the spotlight—it comes from being true to yourself.

He also stays away from drama. When people in the media try to stir up trouble or make false stories, Kylian doesn't argue or get angry. He stays calm and lets his actions speak for him. If someone says something unkind, he responds with class. If someone challenges him, he rises above it and focuses on what he can control—his attitude, his effort, and his performance.

In interviews, Kylian is polite, thoughtful, and respectful. He thanks his fans, appreciates his teammates, and shows gratitude for the people who helped him along the way. He never acts like he's better than others, even though he has achieved more than most players could ever dream of. He believes that every person has value, and he treats everyone—from a young fan asking for an autograph to a reporter asking a question—with kindness.

Staying humble and focused has helped Kylian Mbappé build a career full of success, not just in terms of goals and trophies, but also in the way people respect and admire him. Coaches trust him. Teammates enjoy working with him. Fans from every corner of the world see him as a hero—not just because of what he can do with a ball, but because of who he is as a person. He proves that greatness isn't just about talent. It's about how you carry yourself when you win and how you handle things when you lose. It's about staying true to your values and always striving to be better.

For young people everywhere, Kylian Mbappé is a shining example of what it means to stay humble and focused, even when the world is watching. His journey shows that you can dream big, work hard, and achieve amazing things—but you should never forget to be kind, respectful, and grateful along the way. Whether he's celebrating a goal, helping a child in need, or quietly walking through his neighborhood, Kylian lives with purpose and heart. And that's what makes him not just a football star, but a role model the world can look up to.

Chapter 18: The Olympic Dream

Ever since Kylian Mbappé was a young boy growing up in Bondy, one of his biggest dreams—alongside playing in the World Cup and scoring goals for France—was to one day take part in the Olympic Games. The Olympics, one of the oldest and most celebrated sports events in the world, brings together athletes from every country to compete in a spirit of peace, friendship, and excellence. For Kylian, being part of that global family of athletes wasn't just about winning medals—it was about representing his country with pride, standing alongside athletes from different sports, and living a dream shared by generations of sports lovers.

From an early age, Kylian knew about the Olympics. He saw photos of the opening ceremonies with flags waving and fireworks lighting up the sky. He watched races, matches, and performances by athletes from around the globe. He saw how the Games weren't just about competition—they were about unity, hard work, and pushing the limits of what the human body and spirit could do. For someone as passionate about sports as Kylian, the Olympics felt magical. He imagined what it would be like to walk into the stadium wearing the blue, white, and red of France, hearing the cheers of the crowd, and playing the game he loved as part of something so much bigger than just football.

Although Kylian had already reached some of the highest levels in football—like winning the FIFA World Cup at just 19 and becoming a superstar at clubs like AS Monaco and Paris Saint-Germain—he never gave up on his Olympic dream. Even after becoming a global icon, he made it clear in interviews that the Olympics was something he deeply respected. He once said that the Olympic Games are "the DNA of sport" and that wearing the French colors there would be a huge honor. His words showed how much he admired the history and spirit of the Games.

Kylian's dream of playing in the Olympics became even more meaningful when it was announced that the 2024 Summer Olympics would be held in Paris, his home country. The idea of competing in the Olympics not just anywhere—but in the capital of France, where millions of fans would be cheering on their home teams—was incredibly exciting. It would be like coming full circle for Kylian: from a child playing football in the streets of Bondy to representing his nation on one of the world's biggest stages, right at home.

For football players, the Olympics are a little different from other tournaments. While most football competitions include the very best players of every age, the Olympic football tournament mostly focuses on younger athletes—usually under 23 years old—with just a few older players allowed. Since Kylian is already past that age limit, he would need special permission to join the team. But he didn't let that stop him from hoping and speaking about his desire to be part of the squad. He even said he would rearrange his busy football schedule if it meant getting a chance to play at the Olympics. That's how much it mattered to him.

Kylian's Olympic dream also shows how deeply he cares about his country. He's already proven himself as a national hero, but he doesn't play football just for personal success. He plays to make people proud, to bring joy to fans, and to be part of something greater than himself. That's why he wants to be part of the Olympic team—not for fame or trophies, but for the meaning behind it. He wants to stand with other French athletes, from swimmers and sprinters to gymnasts and judo champions, and celebrate the unity and power of sport.

Even though nothing is guaranteed, and many decisions are made by coaches, clubs, and Olympic committees, Kylian's dream has inspired many. Young athletes in France and around the world are watching closely. They're inspired not just by his incredible goals but by the fact that someone as famous and accomplished as Mbappé still dreams of something more—something that connects him to the heart of the sporting world. It shows that even the biggest stars still have dreams left to chase.

If he were to play in the Olympics, it would be an unforgettable moment. Imagine the stadium packed with fans from every nation. Imagine children watching on TV, seeing Kylian Mbappé take the field not in a World Cup or Champions League match, but at the Olympic Games. The Olympic football tournament may not always get the same attention as other competitions, but if Kylian joins, that could change. His presence would bring new energy and excitement, drawing attention to the Games and inspiring millions to follow the Olympic journey more closely.

Whether he plays or not, Mbappé's respect for the Olympics shines bright. He has always supported French athletes from all sports. On social media, he often celebrates their victories and encourages them before big competitions. He knows how hard they work and how much pressure they face. He understands that the Olympic dream isn't just his—it belongs to runners, rowers, boxers, fencers, and every athlete chasing greatness. That's why he wants to be part of it. Not to be the center of attention, but to be a teammate, a supporter, and a proud French Olympian.

If Kylian gets the chance to join the 2024 Olympic team, he will train just as hard as he does for any other match. He'll give everything on the field, run with all his speed, pass with precision, and play with heart. And if he scores, he won't just be celebrating a goal—he'll be living a dream he's held since childhood. He'll be showing the world that no matter how much you've already achieved, there's always room to dream bigger.

The Olympic dream is a story of hope, unity, and passion. It's about people from different countries coming together to celebrate what we share in common. For Kylian Mbappé, it's a chance to connect his love of football with his love of country, his respect for athletes everywhere, and his belief in the power of sport to bring people together. Whether he's sprinting toward a goal or waving the French flag with other Olympians, Kylian's Olympic dream is something the whole world can admire.

And even if the dream doesn't happen exactly as planned, it will still live on. Because what really matters isn't just being part of the Games—it's the spirit behind the dream. It's the hard work, the passion, the love of sport, and the desire to bring joy to others. And in all those ways, Kylian Mbappé has already shown that he carries the Olympic spirit in his heart, every single day.

Chapter 19: Role Model for the Future

Kylian Mbappé is more than just one of the fastest, most talented football players in the world—he is a shining example of what it means to be a role model for the future. A role model is someone others look up to, not just because they're good at something, but because of who they are, how they treat people, and how they use their success to help others. Young people from all around the world watch Kylian and see someone who is respectful, hardworking, humble, and kind. He's someone who never gives up, even when things get tough, and someone who tries to make the world a better place, one small step at a time.

From the moment he began playing football professionally, Kylian stood out—not only for his incredible speed and amazing goals but also for his positive attitude. When he scores, he celebrates with joy, but he never brags. When his team wins, he smiles and thanks his teammates. And when they lose, he keeps his head high, learns from his mistakes, and comes back stronger. These are just some of the qualities that make him such a strong role model. He shows kids everywhere that success is not just about being the best—it's about giving your best, treating others with respect, and always doing your part.

One of the reasons Kylian is admired by so many is because he never forgot where he came from. He grew up in Bondy, a working-class neighborhood just outside of Paris. It wasn't a rich place, but it was full of strong families, big dreams, and kids who loved to play football. Kylian never acted like he was better than anyone else just because he became famous. In fact, he often returns to Bondy to visit his old schools, playgrounds, and football fields. He talks to kids who have the same dreams he once had and reminds them that they can achieve great things too, no matter where they start in life.

Kylian has also made a big difference through his charity work. He started an organization called "Inspired by KM," which helps children from all kinds of backgrounds find their own paths to success. His foundation gives support to kids who need help with school, sports, or health. He visits hospitals to spend time with children who are sick, bringing smiles to their faces just by showing up and listening to them. He has donated millions of euros to good causes, including money he earned from the 2018 World Cup, which he gave to help disabled and sick children. All of this shows that he cares deeply about others—and that he wants to use his success to lift people up.

Being a role model also means setting a good example, even when it's hard. Kylian has faced pressure, stress, and even criticism, but he has handled it with maturity and grace. He doesn't fight back with anger or shout mean things. Instead, he speaks kindly, stays calm, and focuses on improving himself. He knows that young people are watching, and he wants to show them how to be strong and fair, even in difficult moments. When he missed an important penalty during the 2020 UEFA Euro tournament and received unkind comments, he stayed brave, kept training, and came back with more determination than ever.

Kylian also speaks up for what he believes in. He isn't afraid to talk about fairness, inclusion, and justice. He stands against racism and wants football to be a sport for everyone. He knows that being a good player isn't enough—it's also important to be a good person. He encourages others to stand tall, speak up, and treat everyone equally. That kind of courage is part of what makes him such a powerful role model for the future. He doesn't just play football—he uses his voice to make a difference.

Another way Kylian inspires the next generation is by showing that hard work really pays off. He trains every day, even when he's tired. He listens to his coaches, practices his skills, and studies games to figure out how to improve. He doesn't rely only on talent—he keeps learning and growing. This teaches young people that you don't become great overnight. You have to keep trying, stay focused, and never give up on your dreams. He reminds kids that effort matters just as much as natural ability, and that every challenge is a chance to get better.

Kylian also keeps things real. Even though he's super famous, he stays close to his family, especially his mom, dad, and younger brother, Ethan. He spends time with friends, plays video games, listens to music, and enjoys regular things like any young adult. This shows that you can be successful and still be yourself. He doesn't need to show off or act like a superstar all the time. Instead, he shows that staying true to who you are is one of the most important things of all.

Young athletes who dream of becoming professional players can learn so much from Kylian. They can learn to work hard, be respectful, and lift up others. They can learn that being fast, strong, or skilled is great—but having good character is even better. They can learn that winning isn't everything and that being kind, honest, and generous makes you a real champion. Kylian shows kids that they can shine in their own way, whether they're on a football field, in a classroom, or just trying their best in everyday life.

What makes Kylian truly special is that he inspires not just with his feet but with his heart. Every pass he makes, every goal he scores, and every kind gesture he shows adds to the story of a person who wants to leave the world better than he found it. He's not perfect—no one is—but he keeps trying to grow, learn, and lead in a way that helps others. That's what being a role model is all about.

In every part of the world—whether in big cities or tiny villages, in schools, playgrounds, or football clubs—there are kids who dream because of Kylian Mbappé. They wear his jersey, copy his moves, and try to be just like him. But more than that, they try to be good teammates, kind friends, and strong dreamers, because that's what Kylian teaches through his actions. He shows them that they can be champions not just in games, but in life.

As he continues his journey—scoring more goals, setting new records, and maybe even joining the Olympic Games—Kylian will keep inspiring future generations. His story is proof that you can come from anywhere, dream big, work hard, stay kind, and change the world. And that's why Kylian Mbappé will always be remembered not just as a football superstar, but as a true role model for the future.

Chapter 20: What Comes Next for Mbappé

As Kylian Mbappé continues to grow as a player and a person, one of the biggest questions everyone around the world wonders is: What comes next for Mbappé? After all, he has already achieved so much. He won the FIFA World Cup at just 19 years old. He became a star at AS Monaco and then at Paris Saint-Germain. He played alongside legends like Neymar and Lionel Messi. He scored hat-tricks, broke records, and inspired millions. But even after accomplishing all these things, Kylian isn't done. He's just getting started. There are still so many adventures, challenges, and dreams ahead of him—and each one will shape the next exciting chapter of his journey.

One big part of what comes next for Mbappé is his move to a new club. After many incredible years at PSG, Kylian decided to take the next step in his career by joining a different team. Changing clubs is a big decision for any player, but for someone as talented and well-known as Mbappé, it's even more important. Fans wonder where he'll go, how he'll fit in, and what he'll do on his new team. Wherever he goes, he'll bring his amazing speed, sharp thinking, and goal-scoring magic with him. People are excited to see how he adapts to a new style, new teammates, and a new stadium filled with fans ready to cheer him on.

Playing in a new league will also give Kylian fresh challenges. He might face different kinds of defenders, new strategies, and tougher competition. But challenges like these are what help great players become even greater. Kylian loves to compete and improve, and he knows that the best way to grow is to step outside his comfort zone. He'll learn from his new coaches, build chemistry with his new teammates, and aim to lead his new club to championships. Whether it's scoring goals, providing assists, or setting an example for younger players, he'll be ready to make an impact from day one.

Another exciting thing that may come next is playing in more international tournaments. Kylian has already shined on the world stage, especially in the World Cup. But there are still more trophies to chase. He might lead France in the next World Cup or the European Championship, and maybe even the Olympics. Representing your country is one of the highest honors for an athlete, and Kylian takes it very seriously. He wears the French jersey with pride and gives everything he has for his team and his country. In the years ahead, fans will be watching closely as he helps France compete against the world's best.

Outside of football, Mbappé also has a future filled with exciting possibilities. He has already shown interest in many things beyond the game. He loves fashion and has worked with big brands to design cool outfits and shoes. He enjoys photography and sometimes shares artistic photos on social media. He even thinks about writing books, producing films, or starting businesses that help others. Kylian knows that football won't last forever, so he's preparing for a future where he can use his creativity, intelligence, and kindness to do great things in the world—even after he stops playing.

One of the most important things that will always be part of Kylian's future is helping others. His heart for giving is just as strong as his footwork on the field. Through his charity work and his foundation, "Inspired by KM," he continues to support children, especially those who are sick, disabled, or living in difficult situations. In the future, he may build sports centers, create scholarship programs, or open schools for kids who need more opportunities. He understands that true greatness is not just measured by goals and trophies—but by how many lives you touch. That's why he plans to keep giving back, no matter where his journey takes him.

Kylian may also take on the role of mentor and leader for younger players. As he gains more experience, he'll have more wisdom to share. Just like older players once inspired him, he now inspires the next generation. One day, he might coach a team, manage a club, or even work with youth programs to help kids learn the values of teamwork, discipline, and belief in themselves. He wants young players to feel seen and supported, just as he did when he was growing up in Bondy. Being a leader on and off the pitch will surely be one of the most powerful parts of his future.

Another big question for the future is: can Kylian become the greatest player of all time? People have already compared him to legends like Pelé, Ronaldo, and Messi. But for Mbappé, it's not just about winning awards or breaking records. It's about consistency, humility, and love for the game. If he continues training hard, staying healthy, and growing both as a player and a person, he has a real chance to go down in history as one of the all-time greats. He's already made his mark, but the story is far from over.

As Mbappé gets older, his role in football might also change. Maybe he'll play in different positions, take on new responsibilities, or even switch to leagues in other countries. Some players end up in the Premier League, La Liga, or even Major League Soccer in the U.S. Wherever he ends up, fans will follow him because they know that Kylian brings passion, skill, and excitement to every game. His presence on the pitch is like a spark—he can change the whole rhythm of a match with one sprint, one pass, or one shot.

Kylian's future might also include becoming a voice for important global issues. He already speaks out against racism, unfairness, and inequality. In the years to come, he might work with world leaders, support charities across the globe, or even start campaigns to promote peace, education, and kindness. He has a strong voice, and people listen when he speaks. With his platform, he can help solve real problems and bring hope to millions.

Of course, there will be ups and downs in the future, just like in any journey. There may be injuries, tough matches, or moments of doubt. But Kylian has already shown that he knows how to handle tough times. He stays calm, focuses on what he can control, and keeps moving forward. His ability to learn from mistakes and bounce back stronger is one of the things that makes him a true champion. The road ahead may not always be easy, but Kylian is prepared to walk it with courage and strength.

And one day, far in the future, when Kylian finally hangs up his boots and retires from football, his story will still continue. People will remember him not just for the goals he scored or the trophies he lifted, but for the way he made them feel. For the hope he gave. For the dreams he inspired. For the way he showed that greatness comes from hard work, love, and never forgetting who you are.

So, what comes next for Mbappé? The answer is: anything he dreams of. His future is a wide-open field, full of adventure, growth, and possibility. Whether he's leading France to another World Cup, creating a new business to help children, speaking on big stages, or quietly inspiring a kid who wants to be just like him, Kylian Mbappé will keep moving forward—with speed, heart, and purpose. His story is far from finished. In fact, it's only just beginning.

Epilogue

Kylian Mbappé has already done so much—and he's still just getting started! From scoring in the World Cup to becoming a hero for kids everywhere, his story shows us that talent, hard work, and kindness can take you far. But Mbappé isn't only about goals and trophies. He's also about giving back, staying humble, and believing in the power of dreams.

As you finish this book, remember that your own journey can be just as exciting. Whether it's on the football field, in school, or chasing any dream you love, you have the power to make it happen—just like Kylian did.

The End.